NEW YORK STATE MEN

INDIVIDUAL LIBRARY EDITION

WITH

BIOGRAPHIC STUDIES

CHARACTER PORTRAITS

AND

AUTOGRAPHS

Hon JAMES H. MANNING
EDITOR

THE ALBANY ARGUS ART PRESS
ALBANY, N. Y.— 1921

FREDERICK S. HILLS,
Compiler and Assistant Editor.

New York State Men: Individual Library Edition, With Biographic Studies, Character Portraits And Autographs, Issues 204-213...

Frederick Simon Hills

Nabu Public Domain Reprints:

You are holding a reproduction of an original work published before 1923 that is in the public domain in the United States of America, and possibly other countries. You may freely copy and distribute this work as no entity (individual or corporate) has a copyright on the body of the work. This book may contain prior copyright references, and library stamps (as most of these works were scanned from library copies). These have been scanned and retained as part of the historical artifact.

This book may have occasional imperfections such as missing or blurred pages, poor pictures, errant marks, etc. that were either part of the original artifact, or were introduced by the scanning process. We believe this work is culturally important, and despite the imperfections, have elected to bring it back into print as part of our continuing commitment to the preservation of printed works worldwide. We appreciate your understanding of the imperfections in the preservation process, and hope you enjoy this valuable book.

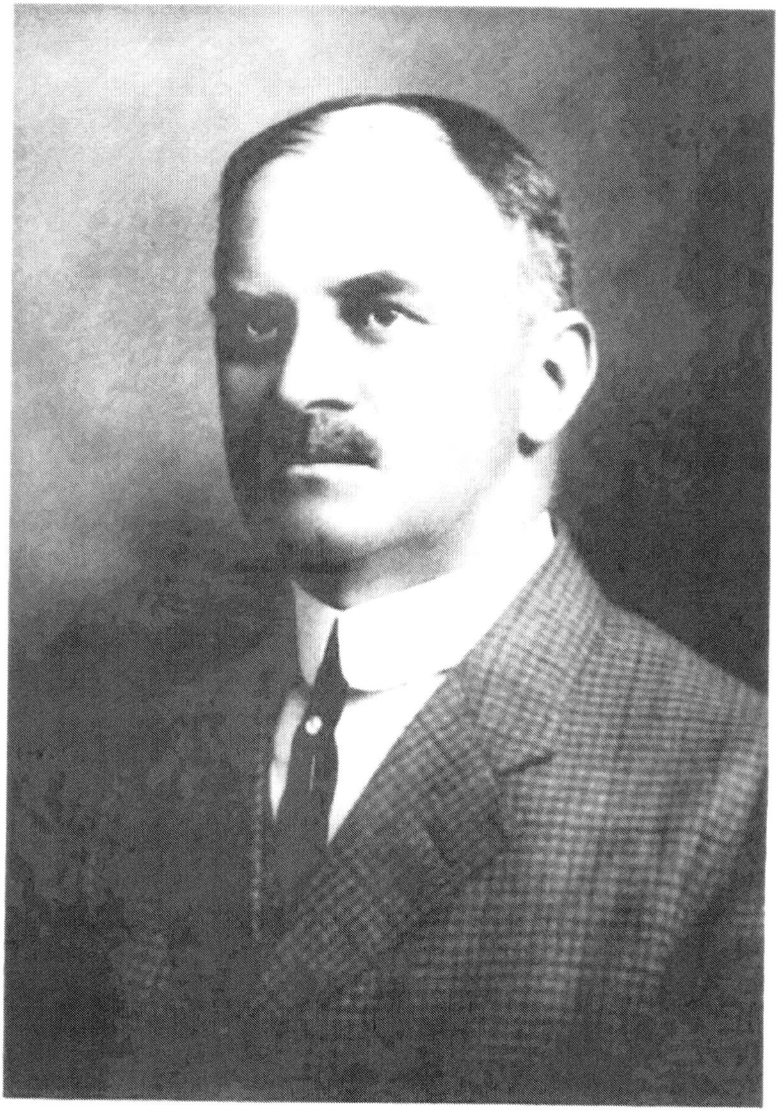

EDWARD JOHN HUSSEY

Edward J. Hussey, banker and philanthropist, who through many years of benevolent activity earned the right to be termed "the friend of the poor," was born in Albany, N. Y., July 25, 1855. He advanced from a clerkship to the vice-presidency of one of the largest banks in Albany, was a director in several others and a leading spirit in many charitable organizations. He resided in Albany all his life, and in his highly successful efforts to make the community better, to promote happiness and alleviate suffering he followed the example set by his worthy father, Nicholas Hussey, Sr., who was in his generation one of the most revered men in Albany and was known as "the father of the Catholic Union," for it was due chiefly to his initiative and liberality that this institution was founded. He came to Albany from Ireland when a boy, built up a prosperous business and died full of years and honor March 16, 1895.

Edward J. Hussey graduated from the Albany Boys' Academy in 1869 and at once entered the National Commercial Bank as a clerk. His fine ability and his devotion to his duties won him steady advancement to teller, discount clerk, assistant cashier, cashier and finally vice-president. His reputation as one of the ablest bankers in the country was well deserved. For many years he was also a trustee of the National Savings Bank of

Albany and one of its vice-presidents. The esteem in which he was held by his associates in the financial field is well expressed in minutes adopted by the Board of Trustees of the National Savings Bank at a special meeting held December 11, 1920, in which it was stated:

"His judgment was sound, his constructive power was along high-minded lines, his loyalty was limitless and his first consideration always was the welfare of mankind. It can be truly said that in life he radiated sunshine and happiness, and in death he bequeathed to his fellow men the peculiar legacy of resplendent example of doing good for others and of rare God-given powers."

Mr. Hussey was for seven years a director of the Municipal Gas Company of Albany, a director of the Morris Plan Company of Albany from its organization, a director of the Home Telephone Company before its absorption by the Bell interests, and treasurer of the Albany Cottage Association. Edward J. Hussey's name officially connected with any business enterprise was a guarantee of its soundness.

Great as was Mr. Hussey's success in the financial world, his character found fullest expression in his deeds of mercy and his promotion of activities for human progress and betterment. There was no form of misfortune that did not appeal to his big heart, and the poor and humble were the special recipients of his sympathy and practical assistance. The mantle of his father fell upon his shoulders, for he succeeded him as chairman of the Particular Council of the Society of St. Vincent de Paul, the perfectly organized Catholic association that covers the entire city of Albany in its ministrations to the needy and makes no discrimination as to creed in its benefactions. For forty-seven years Edward J. Hussey was an indefatigable worker and guide in this society.

Mr. Hussey may be said to have inherited from his father his interest in the Catholic Union of Albany. He was one of its incorporators and for more than thirty years its president. The intellectual, spiritual and physical development of youth was one of his objects, and he made the Union a notable factor in this work. The Board of Directors in minutes adopted at a special meeting on December 10, 1920, truly said of him:

"His counsel was at all times sought and graciously given. During all these years he worked unselfishly and zealously for the success of this organization so dear to his heart. In his passing the Catholic Union of the City of Albany has lost one of its most interested, active and wholesouled members, his friends a cheery and pleasant companion, the city of Albany a citizen of noble ideals and sterling worth."

Mr. Hussey was one of the mainstays of the Home for the Aged of the Little Sisters of the Poor in Albany, to the founding of which many years ago his father contributed invaluable counsel and substantial aid. He was for a long time treasurer of St. Peter's Hospital, his knowledge as a financial expert making him specially helpful in that office. He contributed liberally to its support and some years ago his genius for organization and his abounding energy were largely responsible for the success of a drive for a fund of $100,000 for that institution. Mr.

Hussey was instrumental in establishing the Masterson Home for Poor Children in Albany, and asylums, schools, libraries and all forms of welfare and relief work enlisted his hearty cooperation.

He was one of five children of Nicholas and Anne (O'Connor) Hussey. Mary J., his eldest sister, died March 15, 1919. Captain William M., the oldest brother, for years a commission merchant in Albany, died in 1918. A brother, Nicholas, Jr., died in 1903. Marcella A., the surviving member of the family, resides in Albany.

Edward J. Hussey died in Albany December 10, 1920. His natural nobility, responsive humanity and spotless life endeared him to all who came within the wide circle of his acquaintance, and of him it can be said with peculiar appropriateness,

"None knew him but to love him,
None named him but to praise."

The motives and achievements of his life are admirably summed up in the following brief extracts from resolutions adopted by the officers and trustees, headed by the Rt. Rev. Edmund F. Gibbons, D. D., Bishop of Albany, of the Catholic Charities Aid Association:

"His was an uninterrupted life of charitable deeds and noble services, and he goes to his eternal reward with the benediction of many a fervent prayer of those whom he comforted in their affliction or relieved in their trial. He was one of those rare types of unselfish humanity whose earnest and constant consideration was the alleviation of the ills of the unfortunate. * * * His was a tender and considerate heart, and not only did the sufferings of the lowly appeal to him, but he went in search of the lowly and the unfortunate and brought them comfort and consolation. To Edward J. Hussey, the man with a heart, we turn in kindliest memory, not looking down to where his mortal remains rest, but looking up to that spirit who, with the Great Apostle of Charity, shall remain for the days to come the friend of humanity, and who, serving it, did also serve his God."

WILLIAM JOSEPH BRADLEY

NEW YORK STATE MEN

CPSIA information can be obtained at www.ICGtesting.com
Printed in the USA
BVOW07s1206040314

346526BV00027B/493/P

9 781272 968427